celery

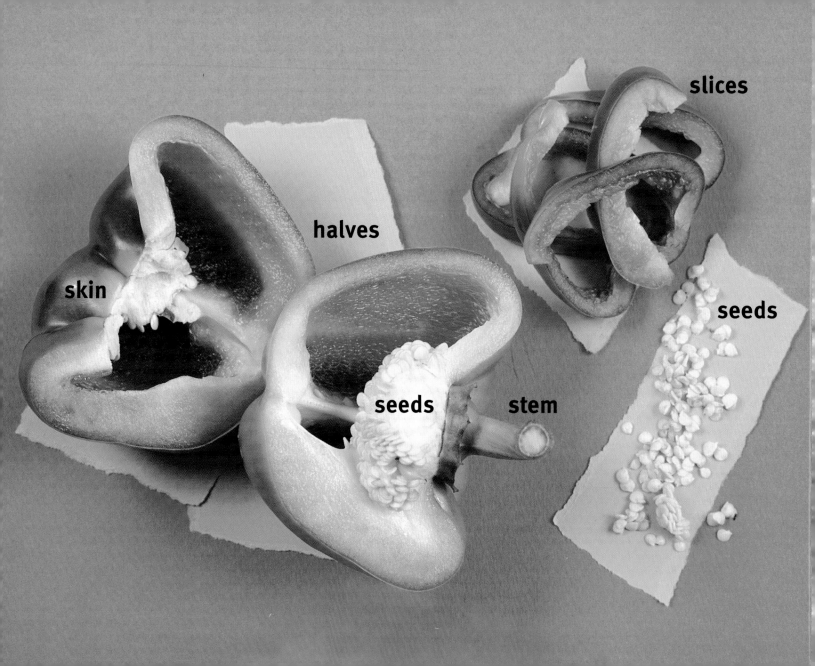

green
pepper

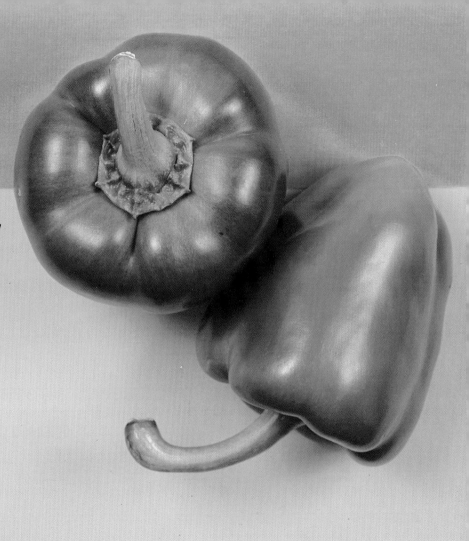

avocado

small and sweet like...

pomegranate

passion fruit

peas

cool and refreshing like...

yoghurt

beansprouts

grapes

cucumber

skin

leaf

half

stalk

root

slices

skin

radish

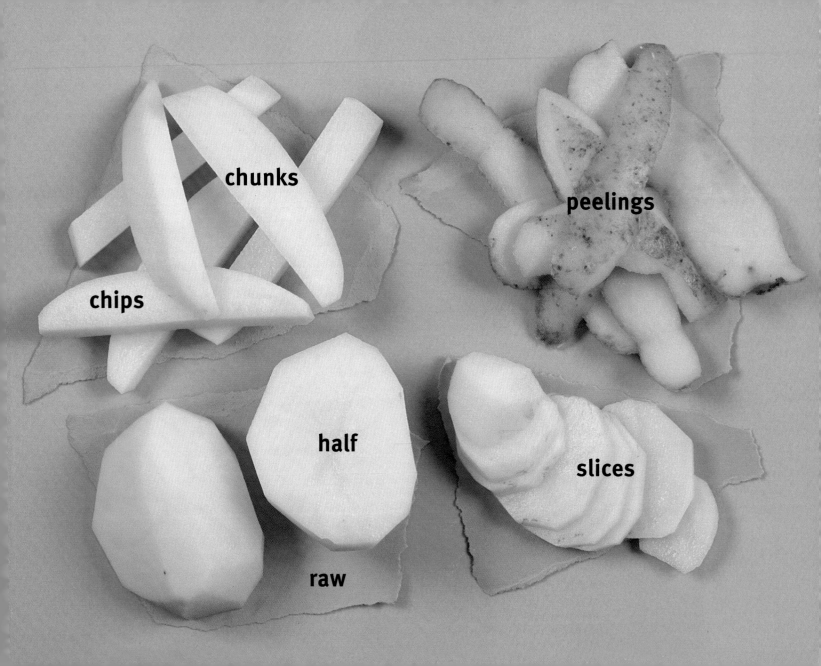

often different like...

pasta

sweet potato

rice

potatoes

Sally Smallwood

Cool as a Cucumber!

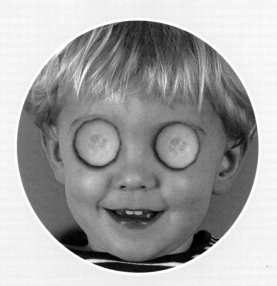

For Joe who always did like his broccoli!

First published in Great Britain in 2002 by Zero To Ten Limited
327 High Street, Slough, Berkshire, SL1 1TX

Publisher: Anna McQuinn
Art Director: Tim Foster
Senior Editor: Simona Sideri
Publishing Assistant: Vikram Parashar

A CIP catalogue record for this book is available from the British Library.

ISBN 1-84089-227-7

Printed in Hong Kong

Picture credits
A-Z Botanical Collection: potatoes, green pepper; Holt Studios: radish,
peas, avocado, mushroom; Photos Horticultural: cucumber, celery.